The Family Bible Study Series

FAMILY BIBLE STUDY SERIES

BOOK SIX

THE BOOK OF REVELATION

Eric C. Dohrmann

WESTBOW
PRESS®
A DIVISION OF THOMAS NELSON
& ZONDERVAN

Scripture quotations marked (NASB) taken from the New American Standard
Bible® (NASB), Copyright © 1960, 1962, 1963, 1968, 1971, 1972, 1973,
1975, 1977, 1995 by The Lockman Foundation
Used by permission. www.Lockman.org

Scripture quotations marked (KJV) taken from the King James Version of the Bible.

Scripture quotations marked (NIV) are taken from the Holy Bible, New
International Version®, NIV®. Copyright © 1973, 1978, 1984, 2011 by Biblica,
Inc.™ Used by permission of Zondervan. All rights reserved worldwide.
www.zondervan.com The "NIV" and "New International Version" are trademarks
registered in the United States Patent and Trademark Office by Biblica, Inc.™

WestBow Press books may be ordered through booksellers or by contacting:

WestBow Press
A Division of Thomas Nelson & Zondervan
1663 Liberty Drive
Bloomington, IN 47403
www.westbowpress.com
1 (866) 928-1240

ISBN: 978-1-9736-6035-4 (sc)
ISBN: 978-1-9736-6034-7 (e)

Print information available on the last page.

WestBow Press rev. date: 04/16/2019

Contents

Revelation

The book of Revelation is appropriately titled—The Revelation of Jesus Christ, as the first few words of the book bring out. The bigger picture of this means the fulfilling and completing all things of God's plan and prophecies in His Son, Jesus Christ (Eph.1:9-12; Rev.19:10; 1 Cor.15:23-28). More specifically also, a number of "revelations of Jesus" comes forth in this book: 1) His Triumphal Character (1:12-16); 2) The Lamb who was slain (5:6-10); 3) The Harvester of the final harvest (14:14-20); and 4) The Triumphant Victorious Warrior and King (19:11-18; see also Zeph.3:14-20). Remarkably and miraculously, add these to Jesus' incarnation, transfiguration and resurrection body, John saw Jesus in seven different appearances in his lifetime—quite the revelations indeed shown to the disciple whom Jesus loved (Jn.21:7, 20)!

Revelation is tied together in four specific visions John received in the Spirit (1:10; 4:2; 17:3; 21:10). All give a specific revelation in God's plan to show His activity and lead to the completion of His everlasting purpose—to fulfill His Family and live with them forever in the New Jerusalem and New Heaven and New Earth (Rev.21, 22; see Book 4 of The Family Bible Studies Series, The

<u>Theology of the Bible—The Family of God</u> for a more complete Bible review on this great work of God throughout time, 41 pages).

Time frame is also a factor in the Book of Revelation—past, present and future (1:19). In 1:10, John says that he was in the Spirit—the general Greek past tense (aorist tense) used here. So, John is writing down his vision in the near recent past for others to read and wonderfully preserved by Almighty God throughout that time since. Presently, John was writing to seven churches in western Asia Minor (western Turkey today). The messages were directed to those seven churches, but the Lord's truths are applicable from that time on, as well (Heb.13:8; Mt.24:35; Jn.17:17. Chapters 4 and 5 present the current worship in heaven (4:8) and the future coming-to-earth-to-reign of God's Lamb and King Jesus (19:11-18), seen in heaven, with all that being played out from chapter six and onward. A sequence of events is more clearly revealed beginning in chapter six with the appearance of the Antichrist (or possibly here his military leader—6:1-4; 13:1-10). Paul gives us a guideline in First Thessalonians, chapters four and five, and Second Thessalonians, chapters one and two (see the commentaries there) that the Antichrist appears after The Rapture of the Church and his "abomination of desolation" occurs during the Great Tribulation (many believe around the middle of those seven years—Dan.9:27; Mt.24:15; 2 Thess.2:3-5). Visions two and three include his brief reign and swift defeat (17:8, 11; 19:19-21).

Rev.1—The word "revelation" means an unveiling or uncovering ("In the ordinary sense, a mystery implies knowledge withheld; its Scriptural significance is truth revealed"—Vine, for the word mystery, used 4 times in Revelation—1:20; 10:7; 17:5, 7). Note God's transmission of this vision—God, to Jesus, through His angel, to John, to His bond-servants (to His <u>many</u> bond-servants, all believers—all those who would hear these words (vss.1-3; 2:29; 22:17-20). The blessing comes to one who reads it (probably the messengers of the churches—2:1, etc.; Mt.11:10) and those who hear this prophecy and keep it (take to heart, guard, heed—apply oneself to it—vs.3; 22:7,9), for the time is near (vs.3; Ps.90:1-4, 2 Pet.3:8,9; Mt.24:44; 1 Cor.7:29-31; Rev.22:6, 7, 10, 18-20; the word "time" means a fixed or definite period, a season—Vine).

John sends this prophecy to the seven churches in Asia Minor (see introduction) and greets them with God's grace and peace vs.4; see the introduction of Romans 1:1-7 for understanding of the greeting of "grace and peace." Note the Trinity referred to here and the description given to each (vss.4, 5; for "first-born of the dead" see the commentary on Col.1:16-19). Great acclamation here given to Jesus—who has freed the believer from their sins (Rom.6:1-11; 8:31-39; Heb.9:26; 10:10-14) and made us to be a kingdom of priests to serve Him forever; and He will receive the glory and dominion forever and ever, (vss.5, 6; 5:9, 10, 12-14; 7:14, 15; 22:3; 1 Pet.2:5, 9, 10). John confirms the Lord's coming and dominion by quoting Dan.7:13 (Mt.24:30) and Zech.12:10—see the full context of Zech.12:10-14 and also, John 19:37; note— <u>every</u> eye will see Him (vs.7; Mt.24:29-31). John reveals that God is the "Alpha and Omega" (vs.8; the first and last letters of the Greek alphabet; we get the word "alphabet" from the first two letters of the Greek alphabet, alpha and beta); see also 1:17; 21:6; 22:13; Is.41:4; 44:6, 7; 46:8-11. The proclamation "Lord God

Almighty" is a great declaration repeated in key passages of the Revelation; see their listings here—1:8; 4:8-11; 11:17; 15:3; 16:7, 14; 19:6, 15, 16; 21:22).

John now introduces his circumstances and his intent of the prophecy (John is mentioned by name four times in the Revelation—1:1, 4, 9; 22:8). The receiver of the Revelation is believed to be the Apostle John and confirmed as so by numerous early church fathers (Unger). He begins by stating himself as a brother in the Lord who is a fellow-sharer of the sufferings and endurance (Greek word; for definition, see the commentary on Heb.12:7) that are in Jesus (vs.9). Patmos is a small island a little ways off the coast of Asia Minor (Turkey today), a little south of Ephesus, between Turkey and Greece in the Aegean Sea. It's rocky and barren terrain was used as a place to banish criminals. John was sent there by the Roman Emperor Domitian in 95 AD (Unger; vs.9).

John records the first of his four visions (see introduction about them) in the Revelation (vss.11-20). He was commanded to write it in a book (vs.11). "The Lord's day" is taken by most to refer to Sunday (vs.10). John heard a loud voice like a trumpet and was told to write out his vision (prophecy) and send it to the seven churches (vss.10, 11). John saw seven golden lampstands (referring to the seven churches) and seven stars (probably the messengers delivering the prophecy to their churches; vss.12, 16, 20, 3; angel can also mean messenger, Mt.11:10). The vision refers to the Son of Man (Jesus, in light of Dan.7:13, 14; also see Rev.14:14), standing in the middle of the churches (vs.13; see Col.1:16-19). The description here of Jesus in the Revelation of this passage is one of Majestic

Victorious character (vss.13-16): the garment from head to feet refers to His royal kingship (vss.13, 5, 6; 17:14; 19:11-16); His golden girdle is His priestly authority (vs.13; Lev.8:7, 13; compare also Rev.15:6); His hair of white wool and eyes as a flame of fire demonstrate His purity and removing impurities and injustices carrying out His righteous judgments (vs.14; 2:18; 15:4; 16: 5, 6; 19:11; Is.9:6,7; 11:4,5); burnished bronze refers to His strength and power (Unger; vs.15); voice like many waters is His strength of command and the large sphere in which it is heard (vs.15; 14:2; 19:6; see also Ps.19:1-11; Ezk.43:2); He judges righteously with His sharp two-edged sword (vs.16; 19:15; Is.11:3-5; 49:1-3; Heb.4:12); and His face shining as the sun shows the glory of God, as coming directly from His throne (vs.16; see the angel in 14:1; see Moses in Ex.34:29-35; 2 Cor.3:7; 4:4-6; Ezk.43:1-5). At the vision John fell at His feet as a dead man (see similar in Dan.10:7-9, 18) and Jesus encourages him that He died and lives forever more (Rm.6:9, 10), and has the keys of death (and overcoming death—Rm.6:1-11) and Hades (where the unbelieving dead await judgment; see Lk.16:23; Rev.20:13). John was then instructed to write the vision and record it, along with the messages to the churches and the things to take place in the future (vss.19, 20).

Rev.2—The Roman Empire was a polytheistic empire, though it allowed in some places persecution to Christians and even death sentences (2:13). Some had allegiance to a main god of worship and others had many ("The city was greatly addicted to idolatry" (Unger, on Pergamum). Most if not all of the seven churches had thriving economies in their cities and some manufactured special products they were noted for (ex., medical salve for the eye in Laodicea, 3:18). Five of the churches needed some kind, of repentance, one was a suffering church (Smyrna) and one was remaining faithful, with promises given to them to come (Philadelphia).

Ephesus (vss.1-7)-The main message that comes with the letter to Ephesus is to not lose your first love (vs.4; Mk.12:29-31). With a good list of positive accomplishments (vss.2, 3), there is one very important "work" they needed to remember as top priority— doing the works in love in serving the Lord—like they did a first (vs.5). Pretty simple task of utmost importance in the midst of busy schedules and activities we face, including oppositions that can occur (vss.2, 3, 6). It needed repentance, as well, showing other things became the main focus (vs.5). Not much is known about the Nicolaitans, but appears to be tied in with idolatry and their sacrifices (vss.6, 14, 15). As the Spirit says these messages to the churches, Jesus wants His church to overcome their trials and focus on love for Him, and the "tree of life" in God's Paradise for His Family to come (vs.7; 22:1-5; Rm.8:31-39).

Smyrna (vss.8-11)—The main central message that comes to the church from the letter to those in Smyrna is "to be faithful unto death" (vs.10). Jesus is our example as given in vs.8—the first and the last, dying for our sins and rose from the dead, and alive forevermore (1:13-18); Heb.9:24-28). They experienced sufferings and poverty (even in a thriving economy) and were spoken out against by the Jews (vs.9). A short trial of suffering was coming to them (vs.10), but their focus was to be on Jesus and His overcomings (Jn.1:5; 16:33), and the "crown of life" in His coming world and reign (2 Tim.4:5, 7, 8; Heb.11:10, 14, 16;

Rev.11:15; 21:1-7), along with all those overcoming and having life in His name (vs.11; 21:5-8; Jn.3:16-21).

Pergamum (vs.12-17)—The teaching to the church of Pergamum is more implied due to strong warning against false teaching there in the area stated to them—cling, hold fast and teach the Word of God (2 Tim.3:16,17); Heb.4:12; Jn.17:17). False teachers, who do not change and teach the word of God will have to face Him who will judge with His sharp two-edged sword (vss.12, 16; 19:13, 15). Killing a faithful Christian witness is also recorded at Pergamum (Antipas, known to be a bishop there—Unger), declared as the place where Satan dwells (vs.13; see the commentary on the introduction to the churches at Revelation 2). Acts of immorality, associated with food sacrificed to idols, similar to the Old Testament teaching of Balaam (vs.14; Num.25:1; 31:15, 16), which seemed to be similar also to the Nicolaitan teaching (vs.15), was often associated with idol worship. This drew the stern reprimand from the Lord with this entering into the church, or He would come and make war against those doing this, if they did not repent and teach God's word (vs.16). Those overcoming this and come to know Jesus, God will give them the "hidden manna" (the manna that comes "inside," not the literal bread as before—see Jn.6:49-51, eternal life through Jesus—The Bread of Life), and a white stone with a new name on it, that only the one receiving it knows (vs.17; see 19:12; name changes are not unusual, examples are Abraham, Sarah, Jacob, to name a few, representing their true character and purpose God has for them); a white stone was used to vote and acquit people in court; plus used as admissions to important feasts (Vine; see 19:7).

Thyatira (vss.18-29)—The Lord gives strong advice to the church to and through those at Thyatira to hold fast to what they have and continue to do God's works until the Lord comes (vss.25, 26). They too had a problem of immorality and things, including foods, sacrificed to idols, while allowing someone similar to Jezebel (see 1 Kg.16:31; 21:25; 2 Kg.9:7) in the Old Testament to teach and deceive with this teaching (vs.20). God commends the church's good deeds (vs.19), but they were permitting this to take place, and would not repent of it (vs.21). So, God's Son, with eyes of a flame of fire and feet like burnished bronze (see 1:14, 15), would bring condemnation upon those committing adultery, with sickness and death to her children, unless they repent of this (vss.22,23). They were trying to make their teaching appear to have a divine connection, but instead (as the Lord said), were teaching (and deceiving with) the "deep things of Satan" (vss.24, 20). Only God knows the depths of the mind and heart (vs.23; Rm.8:27; 1 Cor.2:10; Heb.4:12) and His works will be done and displayed through those in faith, love, endurance and service to Him (vss.19, 26; Jn.3:19-21), as He will give to all according to their deeds (vss.23, 26-29). To those overcoming and keeping His deeds, they will be with Him and reign with Him in His everlasting kingdom, overcoming the darkness, with the Bright and Morning Star (vss.26-29; 22:5, 16; Dan.7:13, 14; Lk.1:31:33 Jn.1:1-5; 16:33).

Rev.3—Sardis (vss.1-6)—Sardis was a church with incomplete deeds (vs.2). They knew what their deeds were (vs.3) and needed to return to them (similar to 2:5, 26), and continue to do God's works (vss.1, 3 6; 2:5, 26). Cults and immorality were also known in their city and affected the "garments" of some (vss.3, 4; see also James 1:27), and so, needed to repent (vs.3). Those not "soiling" their garments will walk with the Lord in white garments, being worthy of that gift (see 6:11; 19:7, 8); along with those who overcome, confessing Jesus as Savior and Lord, Jesus will also confess them before the father and His angels (vss.4-6, a Family tribute).

Philadelphia (vss.7-13)—The church of Philadelphia was a faithful church, given a specific ministry by the Lord to be His testimony to the world. The "key of David" refers to Is.22:15-25 and Eliakim in charge of the royal household, as David's representative (Is.22:15, 20, 22-24). So God gives open doors to represent Him and in His service, too (vss.7-9). For "synagogue of Satan," see 2:9. However God fulfills this verse, see Jn.17:23 (vs.9). God's promise to them (and the church) is to keep them out of (Greek preposition "ek") the hour of testing coming upon the earth (vs.10). This is consistent with the Rapture of the Church and the Great Tribulation to follow (see commentary on 1 Thess.4, 5 and 2 Thess. 1, 2). "Coming quickly" has the meaning that when the events before His coming and including His coming occur, they will take place quickly (see 22:7, 12, 20). For the "crown of life," referring to rewards to the believer, see 2:10; 2 Tim.4:7, 8; 1 Cor.3:10-15; 1 Thess.5:1-11. The reward for overcomers is to be made a "pillar in the temple of God" (vs.12; 7:15; 21:22; 1 Sam.2:8; Ps.75:1-3; Prov.9:1-6; Eph.2:19-22; 1 Tim.3:15, 16). His family will be seen, known and identified as His possession, living in the eternal New Jerusalem together forever with Him (vs.12; 1 Pet.2:9). The message here by the Spirit goes out to all the churches (as with all the messages to the seven churches—vs.13).

Laodicea (vss.14-22)—The Laodicean church here is one that lacked zeal for the Lord, being neither hot or cold spiritually (vss.15, 16, 19). Jesus declares Himself to them to be the "Amen" (by man, meaning "so be it;" by God, "it is so"—Vine), the "Faithful and True Witness" (1:5; 19:11), and the Beginning of the Creation of God (Source or Cause here; vs.14; Jn.1:1-3, 10; Col.1:16, 17). The Lord says because they are not hot or cold, evidenced by their deeds, He is about to spit (literally, vomit them out of His mouth (similar as could happen with some foods – vss15, 16). They were declaring "to be rich" (present tense) and "had become rich" (perfect tense, past completion with present ongoing effects; see Hos.12:8), and had need of nothing (vs.17). The Lord declared to them because of saying these things that they are wretched (Greek word is undergoing a hardening, callus effect), miserable (Greek word is mercy only here without mercy, pitiful), poor (and continuing on so; see 2:9), blind (Greek word for "smoke," here spiritually blind; see Mt.13:13, 16), and naked (needing God's garments—vs.17; 19:7, 8; Is.61:10; Rm.13:14). The Lord is quite gentle in His reproof (Prov.3:11, 12) and offers them some sound advice (the word for "advice" is a collective advice in invitation, a "uniting" in counsel, similar to Is.1:18). His gold is refined by fire (and so, similar process) to become rich (see Prov.3:13-21; Heb.12:5-13); His garments are white ones (3:4, 5; 6:11; 19:7, 8, given for righteous works); and His eyesalve will help one truly see (vs.18; Mt.6:19-23; 13:16; see Lk.16:11-15 for "true riches"). The Lord calls for repentance here and says for them to be zealous for Him (note, no alternative here, as the conflicts above; vss.19; 15-17). The Lord reproves (Jn.16:8) and disciplines and counsels (together with them—vs.18) in love (vs.19; Prov.3:11, 12; Heb.12:5-13). The invitation in vs.20 is primarily evangelistic (and at least a part of all the "overcoming" promises here the Lord gives in the letters to the churches and at large in the Revelation, 1:3), because believers have already invited him to come in and with the descriptions given here (vss.15-17), there must be a great enough need for the Lord to do this (2 Pet.3:8, 9; Eph.1:7-11). In personal invitation given by the Lord also, overcomers may sit down with Him at His throne (an invitation not always granted by rulers on earth in world history), for He grants them to serve and reign with Him (vss.21, 22; 5:9, 10; 7:15; 20:4; 22:5; Dan.7:18).

Rev.4—With the invitation given to the believer to come to the throne of God where Jesus is at the right hand of God (3:21; Heb.1:1-3), the Holy Spirit now takes John there in a heavenly vision to see the continual worship going on around the throne of God. This begins the second vision of the four given to John to write down and pass on to God's servants in the body of Christ (1:1, 2, 11, 19; 4:1, 2). As John sees God on His throne (see also Dan.7:9-14), His appearance is like two different kinds of quartz colors—jasper (blue, green, or rosy tints) and sardius (a deep orange red), with a rainbow, like an emerald, around the throne (remember where we see the rainbow and what it means over the earth, and here, where it comes from (vs.3; Gen.9:12-17; also see Ezk.1:28). Twenty-four unidentified elders and thrones are around the throne, wearing golden crowns (overcoming victory crowns, similar in meaning to the ones given out in the Olympics of that time; vs.4; 2:10; 3:11; 2 Tim.4:7, 8; see also 1 Cor.9:25—same word as in vs.4 for "crown" in the Greek). The peals of thunder and lightning flashes refer to impending judgment to occur (vs.5; 8:5; 11:19; 16:18). The seven Spirits of God refer to the complete composition of the Holy Spirit (vs.5; 1:4; 5:6; see also Is.11:2; Jn.16:8-11). For the "sea of glass" in vs.6, see 15:2; 21:18, 21; Ezk.1:22; Ex.24:9-11). The "living creatures" are identified as "cherubim" in Ezekiel's vision (vs.6; Ezk.10:15, 20; an angelic order (Unger), having to do with protection (Gen.3:24; Ex.25:18-20) and here directing the never ending worship before the throne of God (vs.8). Their appearances represent the dominion of four divisions of God's creation (lion—animal kingdom; calf (young bull)—domestic kingdom; man—God's creation of mankind in His image; and eagle—bird kingdom of God's creation—vs.7). The description given of the "living creatures" fit their purposes well (vs.8), with unending "heavenly" energy and motion giving continual praise and acknowledgement to the Lord God Almighty for His holiness (worth repeating), His eternal nature, and forever continual thanksgiving to Him, who lives forever and ever (worth repeating also—vss. 8,9), sitting upon His throne (Ps.145:13; 90:2). In such declaration, the twenty-four elders fall down before the throne and cast their victory crowns before the One who bought them and brought them their victory, putting them before His throne (vs.10; 5:9, 10). They praise our Lord and our God because He is "worthy" (the greatest worth and value and deserves the acclamation), to receive "glory" (His character and accomplished works) and "honor" (highest esteem and respect) and power (Greek word is His "inherent power"—Vine; vss.8, 11); for He created all things (Gen.1:1; Jn.1:1-3; Rev.3:14), and because of His will (purpose), they continually exist (Greek verb here) and were created (vs.11; Ps.33; Ps.104; Is.46:8-11).

Rev.5—Chapter five of the Revelation continues on with the second vision of the four that John receives, with further developments of the heavenly vision. This continuation focuses on the "Lamb who was slain" (Jesus, vss.6, 9). John sees a book held in God's right hand, written front and back, and sealed up with seven seals (vs.1; compare Dan.8:26; 9:24; 12:4, 9). The seals open up the impending judgments of God, followed by the trumpets and plagues. No one was found in the vision who could open up the book and break the seals (vss.2-4; see Jn. 5:22-29). An elder comes up to John with "good news," "that" the Lamb who was slain" is worthy to open the book and break the seals (vs.5). He is described as the "Lion from the tribe of Judah" (vs.5; see Lk.3:33; Hos.11:10; Is.31:4; Joel 3:16; Amos 1:2) and the "Root of David" (22:16; 2 Sam.7:11-14; Is.9:6, 7; 11:1-5, 10; Jer.23:5, 6; 33:17). He has seven horn (seven the number of completion; horns signifies rulership and kingship—see Is.9:6, 7; Ps.89:17, 18, 24-29) and "seven eyes," showing the Person and work of the Holy Spirit, sent out to the whole earth; vs.7; see 4:5 and the related verses there. The "Lamb" is worthy to take the book, because He has overcome the world (vs.5; Jn.16:33) in the mission of His first coming to earth (Jn.16:22; 17:4; Heb.9:28), to bring salvation to the world and purchase for God (bring into the Family of God) by His shed blood, mankind from every tribe, tongue, people and nation (vs.9), and making them a kingdom of priests to reign with Him upon (or over) the earth (vs.10, 22:5; Dan.7:1-14, 18; 1 Pet.1:17-21; 2:9, 10).

As the Lamb takes the book, the four living creatures and the twenty-four elders bow before the Lamb in worship, each with a harp (playing victory songs in praise and worship to God—vs.8; see 14:2; 15:2) and yet, in solemn reverence, holding golden bowls of incense, representing the prayers of the saints coming up to God's throne (vs.8)—and they will continue to keep coming during the judgments of God unfolding (8:3,4). The song they sing is a new song to the Lamb, declaring His victory and His great accomplishments for God, purchasing believers in Christ from the earth, to serve before God forever, as His Kingdom of priests (vss.9, 10; 1:6; 7:14, 15; 22:3-5). And the myriads (a large vast number) of angels joined in saying loudly their praises to the Lamb (in individual declared praises to Him—vss.11, 12; see also 4:9; Jn.5:21-24; "power" in vs.12 refers to physical strength in total makeup (inner and outer), given and provided by God (Vine), here referring to His strength in His ministry and enduring the cross, paying for the sins of mankind; see also Lk.22:39-44; Heb.5:7; 12:1-3). And then, all created things join in, giving also their individual proclamation of praises to God, including His dominion over them, forever and ever (vs.13; "dominion" here is the Greek word for God's created and manifested power—Vine; 1:8; 4:11); as God, because of the Lamb's overcoming (vss.5-10), is building His Family to be with Him forever and will completely restore the whole world (Rev.21, 22).

Rev.6—As the second vision given to John continues to unfold (4:2), the scene returns back to earth, displaying a "white horse rider" who goes out conquering on the earth. John sees the Lamb open one of the seals on the book and the "living creatures" declare the order to begin God's judgments (vss.1, 16, 17). This is quite widely thought by many to be the Antichrist or his military leader during the Great Tribulation (vss.1, 2; 2 Thess.2:1-12; Mt.24:21; Rev.7:14; see also Dan.11:40-45). The next seal broken shows his "plight to fight" (make war), taking peace from the earth, with the occurrence of war taking place (vss.3, 4). The third seal broken and order given by the third living creature is famine on the earth, represented by a black horse (vs.5). With the Antchrist present and war taking place, prices for some common items to eat reach a ridiculously high and practically unaffordable price (vs.6). "Oil" is olive oil, needed for lamps of that day (Mt.24:1-13) and medicinal healing (Lk.10:34). "Wine" was also medicinal in those times (Lk.10:34) and wartime history shows some military leaders and others under stress consuming more of this on a personal level (but see Eph.5:17, 18). Seal number four reveals and ashen (pale-looking) horse, indicating death occurring on a very large scale in various ways (Hades—the place where the unbelieving dead await final judgment—increases its number during these judgments; vss.7, 8; see Jer.24:10; 29:17-19; Rev.22:17-19; 1:3). The fifth seal opened shows those who were killed for their faithfulness to God's word and their testimony for Him (vs.9; see the "overcomers" in Rev.12:10-12). Blood underneath the altar is where the Old Testament sacrifices were poured (Ex.29:12). They cry out to God for mercy, judgment and revenge for this atrocity (vs.10). God comforts them for the moment by giving them (the Greek here, "each one") a white robe (see 19:7 8; Mt.22:1-14), until to the others, this likewise, takes place and the judgments are completed (vs.11; 7:14-17). The sixth seal of judgment gives us a glimpse at the end of the Great Tribulation (the sixth trumpet and plaque do also—9:13-21; 16:12-16). The words are reminiscent of Jesus' words concerning this time, quoting from Joel 2:10; 3:15 in Mt.24:29 (vs.12) and Is.13:10 and 34:4 (vss.13, 14; see also Jer.4:24; Ezk.38:20; Nahum 1:5-7). Men hiding in the caves recall Is.2:12-22, for they realize it is the time of the wrath of God upon the earth (pretty knowledgeable acclamation made by them here—vss.15-17).

Rev.7—Before the judgments resume and the last seal occurs and the trumpets begin to sound, John observes an interlude here—the sealing of the 144,000 from the tribes of Israel and another scene of worship at the throne of God. Appointed angels have already been stationed by God to hold back the winds from blowing on the earth (vs.1; why? Note the first trumpet coming up in 8:7 upon the earth, so no one could blame this on the wind—or something else; it is the time of God's appointed judgments—vss.2, 3, as the angels wait for their signal to begin their duty, until the 144,000 are sealed by God on their foreheads; see Ex.12:7, 13; Ezk.9:4-6). Note the various tribes that are sealed of Israel, bond-servants of God, (vss.4-8) and their honorable acclamations acknowledged by God, and their duty and dedication to the lamb—see 14:1, 4, 5).

John then sees a great uncountable (to us) multitude before the throne from every tribe, nation, people and tongue (5:9), standing before the throne and the Lamb, wearing white robes, with palm branches in their hand (used only one other time in the New Testament at Jesus' Triumphal Entry into Jerusalem—Jn.12:12,

13; see also Lev. 23:39-43), crying out loudly, declaring, "Salvation to our God, who sits on the throne and to the Lamb" (vss.9,10, remembering 6:9-11). The elders and living creatures join in worship, declaring similar in 5:12, and then add—"be to our God forever and ever;" note, "Amen" begins and ends the acclamation here, meaning "so be it" (forever; vss.11,12). After a moment of "question and answer" who these are before the throne, the elder explains to John they have come out of the Great Tribulation (vs.14; Mt.24:21), and "washed" their robes in the blood of the Lamb, coming to believe and receive Jesus, the Savior and Lord (22:14; 1:5; 3:4; 1 Pet.1:17-21); and they will serve before the throne forever in God's presence and care in heaven, and with their Shepherd, the Lord Jesus, wiping away their tears and leading His people to springs of living waters, with no more hunger or thirst to ever experience again (vss.13-17; 3:12; 21:4; 22:1-3; Is.25:8,9; Jn.7:37, 38).

Rev.8—After seeing what the first six seals revealed, the seventh and last seal comes as a rather surprise at first with its content— silence (vs.1). It is important for us to remember the "rainbow" around the throne and what it means from the heart of God (4:3). God's desire is always salvation for His creation of mankind, made in His image (meaning, a representative figure, (Strongs); see this elaborated more upon in Book 1 of The Family Bible Studies Series, The Family of God—Foundation on page 7; see also James 2:13 and 2 Pet.3:9). God then releases the assignments to the angels with their trumpets given to them (vs.2). The first four trumpets have similarity with the first four plagues in their "target" of God's judgment (1ˢᵗ trumpet—land of the earth, 1ˢᵗ plague—people of the earth; 2ⁿᵈ of both on the sea; 3ʳᵈ of both on springs and rivers; 4ᵗʰ trumpet—sun, moon and starts, 4ᵗʰ plague—on the sun).

Remembering the cry and prayer of the martyrs at the altar in 6:9, 10, God now begins to answer it through His assigned angel in vss.3-5. After many prayers coming up to the throne of God at the "golden altar" (the altar of incense before the throne of God— see Ex.30:1-3), the angel takes fire from it and casts it to the earth, with impending judgment to follow it (vss.4:5; see the commentary on 4:5). The first trumpet burns up a third of the earth, through fire and hail, including grass and trees (remember the "silence" of the wind back at 7:1). The second trumpet, with the fire cast to the earth, turns a third of the sea into blood, also taking out a third of the sea creatures and ships at sea (vss.8, 9). The third trumpet is like a burning torch that strikes a third of rivers and spring waters, making the waters (bitter, called wormwood—a bitter and injurious plant), causing many of mankind to die (vss.10, 11; see Jer.9:15). The fourth trumpet is upon the atmosphere and sky, and darkens a third of the sun, moon and starts, also making dark a third of the day and night (vs.12), as a flying eagle in the atmosphere then gives the warning of three more trumpet blasts to come (vs.13).

Rev.9—Chapter nine contains the fifth and sixth trumpets sounding off. The "star" from heaven falling to the earth is similar to the third trumpet in 8:10. Remember that God is in control of the judgments, with His main goal to bring in the final harvest

(7:14-17; 14:14-16; 2 Pet.3:9). Note the star is also a "him" (vs.1), who was given the key to "the shaft of the abyss;" (abyss occurs seven times in the Revelation—9:1, 2, 11; 11:7; 17:8; 20:1,3; "a deep or bottomless pit, referring to the lower regions as the abode of demons, out of which they can be let loose—Vine; see also Lk.8:31). The effect of the opening appears much like a volcanic eruption (vs.2). The appearance of locusts is similar to Joel 1:4-7; but here demonic powers are with them, not just behind it, including painful scorpion stings on mankind without the seal of God on their foreheads (vss.3, 4). Note no harm is done to the earth, as brought about by the previous trumpets (vs.4). Mankind is not allowed to die with this sting (James 2:13), though they even seek it (vss.5, 6). The locust, looking like horses prepared for battle, is reminiscent of the Day of the Lord that Joel describes in Joel 2:1-11. Their gruesome appearance combines features of man and animal (vss.7, 8). Verse nine describes an army off to war (also see Joel 2:4-9). The sting is allowed for five months (the normal life of a locust in spring-summer life; vs.10), with a demonic power (their hierarchy), as their leader (vs.11; unlike real locust—Prov.30:27).

Warfare continues on with the sixth trumpet and a massive huge army leading the way (vs.16), in the time known as the Day of the Lord (Amos 5:18-20; Zeph.1:7-18; 3:8-20; Is.13:1-16; 24:1-23; Zech.14:1-15). The voice from the golden altar goes back to God going forth to answer the prayers of the ones slain on earth for the Lord who are under the altar there crying out to the Lord for justice on their part (vs.13; 6:9-11; 8:3). This trumpet release of judgment puts to death a third of mankind on the earth (vss.15, 18), by plagues, fire, smoke and brimstone (vs.18). This is done by the destructive force of four angels (demons; see the word "angel" of the abyss used in vs.11), who have been bound at the "great Euphrates River" (vss.14, 15). God's angels in heaven are free and ready to serve Him (7:1; 8:2). Some angels have been bound by God (like in the locked-up abyss, vss.1, 2; see also 1 Pet. 3:19; 2 Pet.2:4; Jude 6) and reserved for judgment, and only released (as this time of judgment) at God's command (vss.1, 2, 14, 15), and all for His purposes only (vs.15; see also 16:12, the sixth plague, working in conjunction with this and the huge massive army in 9:16). This army has much destructive power with it weapons, out of the faces and tails of their "horses" (vss.17-19). Even after this judgment, those remaining still did not repent of the terrible sins they were committing (vss.20, 21). Question remains—is this the end or Armageddon? One can see that this is not the end quite yet, with the "Kings of the east" and the dried up Euphrates River making their way westward (vast majority of commentators I have read agree on this time frame). For fast conquering of the Antichrist (6:1, 2) that leads up to Armageddon, see Dan.11:40-45, as this appears, according to history, yet to come and applies to the Antichrist.

Rev.10—John now sees another strong angel (5:2), this one coming down out heaven ("strong" here as in 5:2 is God's strength given to the recipient as a gift). Who is this angel?—is the natural question that comes up, with this glorious description that John presents to us in vs.1? The answer is just as he is stated—a strong angel from God (the reason this is not Jesus is because Jesus does not need to swear by God, being God Himself, the Second Person of the

Trinity; see Book 1 of The Family Bible Study Series, The Family of God-Foundation, for further helpful study and insights about the character and functions of the Trinity); also, He created the things of heaven and earth referred to here by the angel (Col.1:16-19), and He lives forever and ever (vs.6). The angel's appearance is just like coming from the throne of God to deliver his message (vs.1). He carried with him an opened little book and stood on the land and seal (vs.2, 5, 8; God's dominion; compare 13: 1, 2, 11; see also Dan.9:24 and 12:7 with vss.5-7 here for God's completion of time and events). Seven peals of thunder then spoke, but John was told not to record what was said (vss.3, 4; see Ps.29:3-9). The angel has a very specific and urgent message (note the element of surprise here)—at the seventh trumpet, the mystery of God is finished, having preached this through His servants the prophets (vs.7). What about the "plagues" yet to come (chapter 16)? One can see in 9:20,21, no one else repented; after "plagues" 4 and 5, they did not repent either (16:9,11); at the last, "plague," they blasphemed God because of it (16:21); and when the Harvester comes in 14:14-16, He sweeps His sickle over the earth (and this before the plagues occur)—because the harvest of the earth (literal Greek word)—was dried up (14:15; followed by vs.16). John then takes the little book from the angel's hand and eats it (see also Ezk.2:8-10) and as it was said, it tasted good, but made his stomach bitter (vss.8-10). Yet, John was instructed to continue prophesying about many peoples and nations and tongues and kings (see 16:14; 17:9-15).

Rev.11—Now awaiting the seventh trumpet coming up in vs.15, John receives some instructions on measuring the temple on earth. Seeing that there will be a physical temple for Israel during this time, the question arises about why this comes up here in the Revelation. The next two chapters focus on Israel and Jerusalem (11:8). There is another chapter and verse that tell us about a temple during this time and that is in 2 Thess.2, where the Antichrist's "abomination of desolation" takes place in the temple and desecrates it (2 Thess.2:3, 4; see the commentary there and also in Mt.24:15, 16). This gives us the background for the beginning of chapter eleven here in the Revelation.

John is instructed to measure the temple and the people in it (vs.1). He is told that the holy city (Jerusalem) will be trampled down by the nations for 3 1/2 years (the last part of the Great Tribulation—vs.2). Two witnesses then appear and will prophesy for the 3 1/2 years (vs.3, 4, in fulfillment of Zech.4:11-14). Many speculations have been made about the identity of these two witnesses, since the Scripture is silent about this. Their activities are like the past about Moses and Elijah mentioned in vs.6, yet, some have also offered the suggestion that these may be two prophets of their own time, raised up by God for the prophetic work of that day. God gives them a special protective power they may use if anyone should try to harm them (vs.5, a sowing and reaping principle here—Gal.6:7; Rev.22:12). The spiritual condition of Jerusalem of that time is stated in vs.8, necessitating the prophets ministry there (vss.1, 2, referred to above, and vs.8). When their ministry is finished (God's time), the Antichrist (the beast—see Rev.13:1-10) will war against them (6:1, 2) and kill them (vs.7). If the people have not believed in Jesus' resurrection for them yet, they are about to witness a sensational demonstration of God's power to do so right before their own eyes, followed by a rapture (transportation to heaven) to complete a marvelous miracle and testimony of God's power and hope before them (undoubtedly broadcasted to the rest of the world, as well—a great video to see over and over and over again!). An extended "celebration" about their death occurs there; yet, God performs the "true" and long lasting "celebration" to the people right there, before their very own eyes (and to the world to hear and possibly see then), and especially powerful since they would not bury them, causing great fear in their enemies (vss.11, 12). But, glory is given to the God of heaven, by those (the rest—vs.13) who know God (vss.13, 18). There resurrection was followed by an earthquake and death to 7,000 people in the city (vs.13).

As the seventh angel blows his trumpet, celebration resounds in heaven by loud voices there (vs.15), praising God for bringing His kingdom to the world through Jesus the Messiah, who will reign forever and ever (vs.15; Dan.2:44; 7:13, 14; Lk.1:31-33). How can they begin to celebrate yet? See the angel's message back in 10:7. So, the elders fall on their faces and worship before the Lord God Almighty, the One who continues existing and always did exist (the Greek verbs here mean this), and by His great power (inherent power, the Greek word) has begun to reign (vs.17). They acknowledge to the Lord that this is His time of judgment (wrath; 6:15-17), which will bring the time for all the dead to be judged (Rev.20:11-15) and for the rewards to the prophets and all His people (22:12), and destruction to those destroying the earth (vss.18, 19; Jer.51:25, 26). The "ark of the covenant" represents God's presence, as John see it in God's temple opened up in

23

heaven, with impending judgment (4:5; 8:5) and the last plagues are about to come (vs.19; 16:1-21; the last seal and trumpet point to impending judgment, while the last plague brings the final judgment occurring at the end (16:17-21 and chapters 17-19).

Rev.12—Chapter twelve continues with the emphasis on Israel and the birth of the Messiah through them. Verse 1 refers back to Joseph's dream in Gen.37:9. This leads up to the birth of the Messiah in vs.2 (for the pains experienced, see Mt.2:16-18). The devil's opposition to them is given in quite dramatic detail in vs.3—seven heads refers to the seven mountains (worldly kingdoms) in Rev.17:7,9,10; then, authority of the devil given to the Antichrist (the beast; see that commentary in chapter 13); the ten horns refer to the last kingdom of the world given to the beast (see 17:12); and the seven diadems refers to a "form" of kingship (Lk.4:6) that the devil displays over the seven world kingdoms and their kings (17: 9,10). The tail sweeping away a third of the stars is difficult to see without further information, but if it has to do with angelic warfare (vss.7-10), whatever was casted down would soon be able to return (of the good angels), since what the devil did very soon is done to him (vss.9, 12)—and not allowing him to return to heaven ever again (vss.7-12; 20:1-3; 20:10; see also Dan.8:10). As the devil tried to prevent the birth of the Messiah, God was well ahead of the scheme to prevent that from taking place (vss.4, 5; Mt.2), and the Messiah was successful in His ministry and ascended into the heaven (vs.5; Jn.17:4; Acts 1:9-11; Rev.19:15). Verse 6 shows God's preparation and protection of Israel during the Great Tribulation after the "abomination of desolation" (vss.6,

14; Mt.24:5-21; 2 Thess.2:3, 4). The main battle taking place is in the heavens (vss.7-10; Eph.2:2; 3:8-12; 6:12, 13; Dan.10:13, 20, 21; 12:1), but the devil operates his misuse of authority through many worldly kingdoms (13:2; 17:9-14). And now is casted down to earth during the Great Tribulation with his fallen angels and does some persecution to Israel and the church (vss.13-17), before being bound in the Millennial reign of Christ (20:1,2), let loose then for a brief time before casted into the Lake of Fire forever (20:7-10).

With this the ones in heaven rejoice of the devil finally leaving their domain (vss.10-12). His accusations and persecutions did not stop God's people exercising their faith overcoming him through the blood of Jesus and the words of their testimony in knowing the Lord, even to their final death, however that takes place (12:11). Many will know then that the devils time (including him) is now short (vs.12; Jn.12:31; 16:8-11).

God has always maintained a remnant for Israel (see Book 4 of The Family Bible Studies Series, The Theology of the Bible— The Family of God, for important remnant verses in the Old Testament (pg.23) and the commentary on the New Testament remnant in Romans, chapter 11, about how God has carried this out throughout time). The devil tries again to get rid of Israel, by a flood, but God miraculously opens up the earth to catch the water and circumvent his murderous attack once again (vss.14-16; 4, 5). The devil was enraged and went off to persecute those keeping God's commandments and having the testimony of Jesus (vss.17, 11; 19:11; "enraged" is an abiding condition of the mind, often with a view to take revenge—Vine; 12:11).

Rev.13—John now is given some of the activities and description of the Antichrist and false prophet of The Great Tribulation. For standing on the seashore, see Dan.7:2-8. The description of the beast is similar to 12:3 (see that commentary for similar explanation as here), as the devil transfers his authority to him (vss.1, 2, 4; see Dan.7:4-6 for the description—the kingdom that took away Israel's kingdom (Babylon) and the two worldly kingdoms that followed them (Persia and Greece; Dan.4, 8). The "head as if slain" in vs.3, called his "fatal wound" (of the sword in vs.14), from our perspective before the event, could be real (since he is a man of war himself—6:1-4; 13:7), could be an assassination attempt, or possibly a conspiracy plot (set up) to get the people to follow the Antichrist (vss.3, 4, 7, 8, noting the lack of harvest on the earth then, vs.8; 10;7; 11:15-18, though the saints are on the earth, vs.7; 12:11, 12). For his blasphemous statements and rebellion for 3 1/2 years (vss.5, 6), see the "little horn" in Dan.7:8, 21-27. For "captivity" and the "sword," see likewise in Jer.15:2; Rev.22:10-15. Endurance is what the saints need to pray for (see the definition in James chapter one and Heb.10:36, 37) and read the Bible a lot (vs.10; 1:3; 22:7).

The false prophet exercises the satanic given authority of the Anti-Christ, and looks lamb-like, but speaks as a dragon (vss.11, 12, 2, 5). His job is to "make" the people worship the beast (vs.2; see Dan.2, 3; Rev. 12:11, 12). He even performs great signs, in all deception of wickedness, power and false wonders (vss.13, 14; 16:13, 14; 19:20; 2 Thess.2:8-12; see also Lk.10:17-20). Through a "false resurrection" of the Antichrist, the false prophet tells those dwelling on the earth to make an "image" to the beast (vss.14,

15). They make it look "alive" (false creation to "look" man-like and "speak" like mankind), so that those who do not worship the beast would be killed (vss.14, 15). The false prophet "makes" (the Greek word here, possibly in conjunction with the image of the beast) the people take a mark on their right hand or forehead in order to buy or sell—needing either the mark, name of the beast or number of his name to do so (vss.16, 17; many alphabets have numerical equivalents to them, example, A=1, B=2 and so on). The word "calculate" means "to count," taken from the Greek word "a stone," which was how counting then was often done (by stones or pebbles, voting and court decisions made, for example—Vine; see Acts 26:10). Greek and Hebrew that the Bible was written in have numerical equivalents. Time will tell when the Antichrist appears how his name and numerical equivalents will work out (vs.18).

Rev.14—The fourteenth chapter of the Revelation of Jesus Christ begins with a scene on the earth, followed by a song from heaven (vss. 1, 2). The scene in vs.1 is on Mt. Zion (the western ridge of Jerusalem, then referred to the whole city (Unger); see this in Is.2:1-4; Is.1:27; Ps.48). The picture presented to us here appears to be the start of Christ's millennial reign (vs.1; 11:15; 12:10) in Jerusalem. The 144,000 have come through the Great Tribulation, having the Father's name and the name of His Son Jesus on their foreheads, as God's possession and protection, chosen as "first fruits" to Him as His witness and service during the Great Tribulation (vss.1, 4, 5; 7:4-8; see some of that celebration during this time frame also in Is.25:6-12). Note too they follow the Lamb wherever He goes, indicating the Lord back on the earth, during His second coming and reign on the earth (vs.4; Rev.20:1-6, in light of the declaration in 11:15). They are declared to have excellent character traits to serve the Lord, including no defilement with women (chaste behavior and conduct; the Greek word is "parthenos," the word for a virgin for females, primarily, in Greek); they are "blameless" (without fault—vss.4, 5). In a very honorable tribute, it appears, at least with them in mind, a new song is sung in heaven by the huge multitude there, singing in celebration on their harps, in joyful choral festivity (vs.2, 3; 5:8; 15:2; see similar multitude description in 19:6), which only the 144,000, purchased from the earth (5:9, 10), could learn the song on the earth (vs.3).

Three angels now appear each proclaiming their own individual message to those on the earth. The first declares the "eternal Gospel" to all mankind, giving charge to fear (reverence) God and give Him the glory, who made heaven and earth, including the sea and springs of waters, and to worship Him, for the time of His judgment has come (vss.7, 8; for the eternal Gospel, see 1 Pet.1:25, finishing up God's plan of the Gospel through the prophets and carried on into and through the Millennium and its truth forever and ever; Mt.24:35). The next angel announces the fall of Babylon forever—from the time it became the first kingdom on earth through Nimrod (Gen.10:8-14; 11:4) and took away Israel's kingdom and nation in 586 BC, to its final attempt to have a world kingdom revived in the Great Tribulation (Rev.16-18; see Zech.5; Jer.51:24-26)—they and all the worldly kingdoms will fall, not ever to be found again, with the Lord reigning on the earth, because of all the immorality and fornication they brought on the earth (vs.8; 18:1-24; Dan.2:44, 45). The third angel proclaims God's wrath on anyone who takes the mark of the beast during this time he is on earth (vss.9-11; 13:12, 15-17). The result is eternal torment forever with fire and brimstone, having no rest day or night, who worship the beast (vss.9-11, 7). As John endured and persevered for the Lord (1:9), the saints are called to seek God for His strength and endurance and do likewise (vs.12).

Then, John records another vision of the "son of man" (Jesus; vs.14; 1:13; Dan.7:13, 14; see the introduction to Revelation for the "visions" of Jesus in the Revelation). Here Jesus is seen as the Great Harvester, swinging a sickle over the earth to reap it (harvest it); but as vs.15 states, the harvest is (literally) dried up (New American Standard Bible has the words in the margin outside this verse, "has become dry;" see previous commentary on 10:7). Verse 16 declares the earth was reaped, and the time of God's judgment has come (vss.15, 7; Joel 3:13). And so, the last angel here swings his sickle to bring God's judgment on the unbelief and wickedness of the earth and gather those under God's judgment for the final war (Armageddon) of His wrath before the Lord returns for His Millennial reign, vss.17-20; (9:20,21; 15:1; 21:8; 22:14,15; Jn.3:16-21). With the end soon coming before the Lord's return, the believers who die from that time on are encouraged that they will enter God's rest in heaven, resting from their labors, and rewarded for their good deeds (vs.13; 1 Cor.3:10-15; Eph.6:7, 8).

Rev.15—As John now sees the seven angels ready with the last seven plagues of judgment about to come upon the earth, he declares another (12:1) great and marvelous sign in heaven (vs.1). He also sees those who were victorious over the beast, his image and his name (7:14-17), playing their victory songs, standing on a "sea of glass" (see the commentary on 4:6 for the sea of glass; for their harps, see previously at 5:8 and 14:2). As John sees this, they (in his vision) "are singing" (present tense) the song of Moses (Ex.15:1-18), the bond-servant of God, and the song of the Lamb (5:9, 10; note also vss.11-14 there), giving great praise and attribution to the Lord in vss.3, 4. They draw from several Old Testament sources (see Dt.32:3, 4; Jer.10:6, 7; Lev.19:2; Ps.86:9, 10; Rev.16:5, 6; 6:9-11; 19:8; for the wonderful proclamation and tribute to "The Lord God Almighty" in the Revelation, see their listings in 1:8).

John next sees the temple of the tabernacle of testimony opened in heaven (vs.5; see Num.1:50-53; Heb.8:5) and the angels who had the seven plagues. They wear linen, bright and clean (compare 19:8) and golden girdles around their breasts (vs.6; see commentary on 1:13, 14). The angels received the golden bowls of the wrath of God, who lives forever and ever, as the temple filled with smoke from the glory of God (Ex.19:18; Is.6:4); and no one could enter the temple till the plagues were finished (vss.7,8).

Rev.16—All the seven plagues cast upon the earth are contained in chapter sixteen. A voice from the temple commands them to go and proceed with them (vs.1). The first one is a malignant sore cast upon those who took the mark of the beast and worshipped his image instead of God (vs.2; see 14:7-11; only other place found for the word "sore" outside this chapter is in Lk.16:21 about Lazarus, visiting the rich man). The second plague is judgment poured on the sea (probably universal here since all the major seas and oceans around the world are interconnected), and they became blood like that of a dead man, killing every living thing in the sea (vs.3; see 8:8, 9). The third angel poured out his bowl on the rivers and springs of water (major drinking sources for most—see Ex.7:17-21) and they became blood, also (vs.4; see 8:10, 11). The angel of the waters declares God's righteous judgment here (15:3), giving back blood to drink to those who killed (took the blood) of saints and prophets of God—that they deserve it (vss.5, 6; 6:9-11). Then finally, the ones who were killed for their faithfulness to the Lord and His word, and have been waiting for the Lord's righteous judgment and retribution to come on their behalf, chime in convincingly with the angel's declaration to the Lord God Almighty, that there is not ever a doubt that His judgments are true and righteous (vss.7, 5; 6:9-11). The fourth angel poured his bowl on the sun, allowing it to scorch men with fire and intense heat. They reacted by blaspheming God and not repenting of their sins, and so, to give Him glory (note the negative responses to the last three plagues—vss.8, 9, 11, 21; 14:7). The fifth angel poured forth his bowl on the throne and kingdom of the beast and it became darkness (see 8:12; Ex.10:21-23). The people gnawed their tongues and felt the pains from their sores (vs.2; note, from their own caused pain, refusing to repent of their deeds and worship God, and instead, entering in these judgments of God; vss.10, 11; 9:20, 21; 14:7-11). The sixth angel pours out his bowl on the great river Euphrates (current central Iraq; see Is.11:15,16—the river was right in the middle of the Assyrian empire and note this is primarily for the remnant of Israel, the positive end here). The kings of the east and the kings of the world are being gathered together by demons (vss.13, 14) for the war of the great day of God the Almighty (see Zeph.1:14-18; Joel 3:9-17; Rev.17:14) at Armageddon (meaning "mound of Megiddo," a little south of Nazareth and west of Nain (Lk.7:11), southwest of the Sea of Galilee; the valley above it, the plain of Jezreel (or the Greek modification name—plain of Esdraelon), is 20 miles long and 14 miles wide—Unger; vss.12-14, 16). The Lord comes as a thief, and man, not knowing the day or hour (see Mt.24:36-44), yet is to know the "season" (signs) of the Lord's second coming (Mt.24:32-35, 4-14; 1 Thess.5:1-11). For the garments, see 3:3-6, 18-22; vs.15. The last plague poured out by the seventh angel is upon the air, where Satan and his demons were once allowed to roam, will finally be casted into the lake of fire, forever (vs.17; 20:2, 7, 10; Eph.2:2; Jn.16:8-11). A voice from heaven said, "It is done," referring to God's completion of the judgments before the Lord Jesus returns to earth (seals, trumpets and plagues; vs.17; see 15:8). The flashes of lighting and thunder roars occur at the end of each judgment (seals—8:5; trumpets—11:19; and here, the last plague and final judgment completion), all showing impending judgment coming; also, see the beginning of all these warnings in 4:5. Here in the last plague, a great earthquake as never seen before ("so great and mighty"—vs.18) occurs and splits the great city of Babylon, called Babylon, into three parts (vs.19; 14:8; 17:18; 18:10, 16, 19), as God remembers it's abominations, sins and impending judgment (vss.19, 18; 17:5; 18:2-8). The islands and mountains disappearing recalls the sixth seal pointing to the end of the judgments (vs.20; 6:12-17; see also Heb.12:26, 27), along with huge hail taking place (a talent was somewhere between 75-100 pounds). Those not believing in God or worshipping Him (14:6, 7) blasphemed (spoke evil about or toward—see 13:5, 6) God, because of the hail and the plague was so exceedingly great (vs.21).

Rev.17—As people read this chapter of the Revelation, they often wonder—how does Babylon come back into the picture now in the end times before the Lord's return? The answer is in its history trends and Biblical prophecy to be yet completed.

Note its history—First kingdom ever on earth through Nimrod (Gen.10:8-10); its city and the "Tower of Babel," rebelling against God's command (Gen.1:28; 9:7) to establish their own kingdom (Gen.11:1-9); declining, then building up again around 1700 BC with Hammurabi; declined quite quickly through defeat from other countries, including Assyria till they rose again through Nebuchadnezzar the first (1126-1105 BC). The Assyrians routed Babylon again and defeated them in 1027 BC; "tugs of war" continued between the two till 625 BC and Nabopolassar became king of the "new Babylonian era," followed by his son, Nebuchadnessar the second of the Book of Daniel; he destroyed Israel's Jerusalem in 586 BC (see the Book of Habakkuk in the Old Testament); the Persians then destroyed Babylon in 539-538 BC, before Alexander the Great took over them and controlled Babylon in 323 BC, which led to Babylon's diminishing and decline—for the time being in history, anyway (contributive dates and history from Unger's Bible Dictionary). So what then remains of this vast and wide-spread impact that this kingdom and people have had on history?

Note their legacy—they "pop up" and decline…and "pop up"

again and decline again. Will they "pop up" again? The Bible says "yes" and God is not through with them yet (see also Zech.5 and Jer.50, 51), because of what "abominations" they brought on the earth (Rev.17:5—"the mother of harlots"), and still do and will be finally judged by God (Rev.16-18).

Zechariah and Haggai were contemporary prophets for their time, <u>after</u> the Persians took over Babylon. Unger says his last prophecy (not including the latter half of his book) was around 518 BC, twenty years after Persia defeated Babylon and began its empire. In Zechariah's vision in chapter five, he sees a bushel basket called "wickedness." Two women with wings lift it up and carry it to the land of Shinar, the plain of Shinar, the land of Babylonia. It says a temple will be built for her and then she will be placed on her own pedestal (support for a statue, from the Hebrew word "to set up" or "place something on"—Strongs). Sounds like idolatry all over again—fitting in with the Book of Revelation (Zech.5:5-11; Dan.2, 3; Rev.13, 14, 17, 18).

John now receives the third vision in the Revelation he writes down and records for us ("in the Spirit" he was carried away; see similar in Ezk.11:1). One of the angels of the bowls of plagues guides him to see "the great harlot," reigning on the earth (vss.1, 5, 15, 18). She has affected ("infected") many kings and people on the earth with her immorality (vs.2). The woman (Babylon— vss.5, 18) sits on a scarlet beast (the Antichrist—6:1-4; 13:1-10; 18:24), full of blasphemous names (13:5, 6), having seven heads and ten horns (explained in vss.9-13; vs.3). The "harlot" is adorned in royalty—clothes and jewelry—and had a gold cup of her abominations of immorality in her hand (i.e., ready to pour it out, like God does the plagues; vs.4; 18:2, 3). In similar style as God did to His people (7:2-4), here a "mystery" (revealed by God—remember her history; see Rev.1 for the word mystery), a name on her forehead—Babylon the great (it has been around awhile), "Mother of harlots" and the abominations of the earth, including blood of the saints, and witnesses of Jesus, vss. 5,6 (history past and presents bears this out—Dan.2, 3; Rev.6:1-4; 9-11; 13:1-18). The angel next reveals the "mystery" (that is, God reveals more about it—vs.7). He says the beast was, and is not and comes out of the abyss (for which see the commentary at the beginning of chapter nine; 11:7) and goes to destruction (vss.8, 11; Dan.9:27; 11:40-45; some say it is someone of the past or an impersonator of one in the past, or a takeoff of 13:3, 12, 14; see 2 Thess.2:8-12). The angel says the seven heads on the beast (vs.3) are seven mountains, which the woman sits (eight times in the Revelation the Greek word here translates it "mountains," referring to the kingdoms of the kings here in vs.10—"and they are seven kings;" see Dan.2 and Is.2). Babylon is responsible from the start of their first kingdom (Gen.10), all the way to their "pop up" ending, of the abominations of the earth (vss.4, 5; 18:2, 3) in the end times. They are also responsible for the starting and taking away of Israel's kingdom and capital city, Jerusalem, in 586 BC. Other kingdoms followed (called "the time of the Gentiles" (Lk.21:24)—Persia, Greece, Egypt and Assyrian kingdoms (see Dan.11—stated as the north and the south kingdoms then), followed by Rome that took over Palestine in 63 AD, (Unger), adding to their long dynasty of empire rule; kingdoms after this had nowhere near the reign and impact that Rome did in the world for over 14 centuries. The seventh is Babylon here in chapters 17 and 18. The beast only remains a little while (vss.9, 10; 13:5). He is also an "eighth" king, taking his rule with an alliance of 10 other kings, who give him their authority (eighth kingdom) for an even shorter period of time (vss.11-13). They all wage war against the Lamb, who will defeat them in His return to earth to rule and reign (vs.14; 1:5; 19:11-16). The ones with Him are His armies (the single article in the Greek include "called, chosen and faithful" together as one; not all fit this description, as much as we might like to think otherwise; see also His specific "armies" in 19:14; the Lord's main message of those who return with Him are His holy angels (Mt.16:27; 25:31; 1 Thess.3:13—to fit with the other Scriptures the Greek word "holy ones" here should be translated "holy ones" or angels; see also 2 Thess.1:7).

The angel goes on to explain the large vastness of Babylon's rule in the end times (vss.15, 18). Verse 16 says the ten kings who joined up with the beast to form the "eighth" kingdom (vss.11-13) will, along with the beast, turn against Babylon and burn it up to demonstrate their power as a new united alliance and kingdom (and fulfill God's word; see this prophecy in the Old Testament in the context of Babylon's destruction in Is.14:4, 18-22; also Jer.51:24-26, 56; Rev.18:4-6). Babylon thus receives its judgment and final removal from the earth (14:8; 18:2), as God executes His purposes and His prophetic word to put worldly kingdoms to an end and bring in the everlasting rule of His Son, King Jesus (vs.17; Lk.1:31-33; Rev.1:5, 6; 5:9, 10; 11:15; 19:11-16; 20:1-6; Is.46:8-11).

Rev.18—John is now given the vision of Babylon's destruction, its city and final end to its kingdom. One can see why after reading this chapter, especially vss.3, 24, and the previous chapter. He begins with the frequent words "after these things" (vs.1; 19:1). These words occur ten times in the Revelation, showing the continuation and sequence of events that John saw to record for Scripture. He sees another angel with strong authority and illuminating the earth with his glory (on his mission from God—vs.1). He declares that Babylon is fallen (see 14:8 for the preliminary announcement) and has become a dwelling place of demons and unclean and hated birds (vs.2; Jer.50:39; 51:37). The reason for it was given back in 17:4-6 in the description of Babylon, and now the kings and merchants of the earth are declared responsible with it, joining in its luxurious (living "wantingly") lifestyle (vs.3). God's people are instructed to stay away and out of their way of life and their sins, which have piled up to heaven, so as not to receive her plaques, for God has remembered their sins (vss.4, 5; 14:8; 16:19; Jer.51:9, 45). Babylon will be paid back double ("double unto her double according to her works"—KJ) for what she did to others, glorifying herself in her luxury (verb "luxury" of the noun in vs.3), living as a "worldly" queen (vss.6, 7; see the prophecy in Is.47:8-11 about Babylon; also Jer.50:15, 29; 51:56). For this, Babylon will be burned up in a single day (three times mentioned in "one hour," which in today's age may be literal), for God who judges her is strong (vss.8, 10, 17, 19; 17:16).

Three main groups of leaders responsible for committing these actions are—the kings of the earth, the merchants of the earth, shipmasters, all those traveling by sea, sailors and all those making their living by the sea (vss.9, 11, 17). Kings will lament and weep, watching Babylon burning, in fear of her torment, seeing the judgment take place (vss.9, 10). Merchants will lose their vast amount of various cargos, including animals, slaves and human lives involved (vss.11-13), along with all their own luxuries (vs.14). They react as the kings did in vs.10, seeing all the valuable things of their world they "depended" on, gone in smoke in "one hour" (vss.14-17). Those out at sea watch the "great city" (called by them all— vss.10, 16, 18, 19, 21) burning in smoke, where they live and deliver their products and became rich by the abundance of them—being destroyed in "one hour" (vss.17-19). Yet, the saints, apostles and prophets rejoice, because God has brought His judgment upon her ("for the way she treated you"—NIV; 6:9-11); vss.20, 24; 13:7; 16:5, 6; 17:3-6). Then a strong angel appears (see 5:2; 10:1) and fulfills the prophecy in declaration of Jer.51:62-64, showing how Babylon has disappeared and not to be found any longer (Jer.50:39)—throwing a millstone (used for grinding grains and usually turned by an animal—Vine) into the sea (with a rush, the Greek word here), taking all its various "lifestyles" (music, culture, crafts, business, manufacturing, marriages, etc.) with it (the Greek uses the emphatic negative, (two negative two letter words), to declare the final certainty of its disappearance, four times in vss.22, 23); for all the nations were deceived by Babylon's sorcery (Greek word is "pharmakeia," the use of drugs, that can also lead to sorcery; see this in 9:21, also), and in her was found the blood of prophets and saints who were killed on the earth (vs.24; 6:9-11; 13:7; 16:4-7; 17:3-6), and so, judged according to what they deserved (vss.5-8; 16:4-7; 19:1,2).

Rev.19—With the "great harlot" judged by God (17:5; 18:5, 6), the Lord Jesus is now about to return to earth, for the final judgment of the earth and begin His millennial reign. Four "hallelujahs" ("Praise the Lord") occur in heaven: first, for His righteous and true judgments on the great harlot, corrupting the earth with her immorality and taking the life of some of God's servants; for salvation, glory and power all come from the Lord (vss.1,2; 7:10; 12:10; 16:7; Dt.32; 4, 43; Ps.19:9); second, the judgment given the "great harlot" is eternal torment (vss.3, 20; 14:9-11; 16:5-7); third, the twenty-four elders and four living creatures around the throne join in worship and affirm the declarations with their "Amen" (so be it; remember their contributions in 5:8 and God's faithful answers—vss.1-4); a voice from the throne goes forth to God's servants in call to praise Him, those who revere Him, small and great, in unison with the moment at hand, and also knowing His supper is about to occur and the time to give them their rewards is soon to take place (vss.5, 7, 8; 11:18; 22:12); and the fourth "hallelujah" declares praise to the Lord our God Almighty because He reigns (vs.6; the Greek verb is past simple tense here and so, He "reigned," i.e., He won the victory, and is the Victor, all along—Col.2:13-15; Rev.1:17, 18; 19:11-21; Zeph.3:14-20; Is.52:7-10). This also is the introduction to the Marriage Supper of the Lamb (vss.7-9). People wonder and discuss in these four verses about where the Marriage Supper of the Lamb takes place. Looking over the context of these verses with the Book of the Revelation and any other related prophecy passages, I will share six reasons why I believe it occurs in heaven and also give a seventh proposition on how it may, in some capacity at least, carry over to the earth as well: 1) the "Hallelujahs" in this chapter are taken together beginning in heaven (vs.1) with no declared change of location going into the fourth one; 2) the declaration "Lord God Almighty" occurs, seven times in the book, starting off by God Himself (1:8), one a reference to Him (21:22) and all the rest in strong affirmation to the Lord for who He is and what He has done in outward proclamation of worship in heaven (1:8; 4; 4:8-11; 11:17; 15:3; 16:7; 19:6); 3) the setting and description given in 19:6 is the same description given to us in 14:2 of the worship in heaven, minus the harps there for that context; 4) the praise and proclamation of "our Lord God Almighty reigns" recalls this great declaration from Is.52:7-10; this proclamation was given to God back at the seventh trumpet (11:15), as the angel disclosed this in 10:7. With the harvest now in (see the commentary on 14:14-16), this fulfills Jesus' statement at the Lord's Supper to the Apostles in Lk.22:15, 16. His promise is carried over in that chapter to vss.28-30, of them eating at His table and sitting on thrones judging the twelve tribes of Israel, which could only happen with them in heaven, where they are; 5) the "fine linen" given to the saints for their righteous deeds done unto the Lord in vs.8 are the same "linen" (and Greek word) that the Lord's armies wear in heaven (19:14); 6) with these "wedding clothes" in mind, this would put the "marriage feast" in Mt.22:1-14 in heaven, the point being there that one must come into the Kingdom God's way through the spiritual birth (Jn.1:12,13) and eventually with wearing His wedding clothes for the Bride (the believers) that the Lord gives them for the Marriage Supper of the Lamb (19:8); 7) it appears that this may carry over to some degree on earth, also, according to the promise given and exhortations stressed here to the believers and their faithful service to Him, when Jesus returns to earth (see Lk.12:35-40; Mt.25:1-13).

John in his reverence bows at the angel's feet but the angel will not allow it (vs.10) and reminds John to worship God (similar to 22:8, 9), for Jesus' testimony is the spirit of prophecy (here a descriptive genitive in the Greek; prophecy is the kind of spirit declared here, a telling forth of God's word, as Jesus is—the Word of God—vss.10, 13; Jn.1:1, 18), and so, to worship God.

John now sees heaven opened (4:1; Mt.3:16, 17) and Jesus on His white victory horse (see the delusion in 6:2), coming to conquer over sin and wickedness in the earth and rule and reign in His kingdom of righteousness (vss.11-21; Is.9:6, 7; 11:1-5; 49:7; 63:1-6; Ps.2). The description of the Lord returning here are fulfillments of many prophecies. "Faithful and True" recall the Lord's fulfilled ministry on earth (Jn.1:14, 17; 8:29, 30; 14:6; 17:4; Rev.1:5; 3:14), and righteously He judges and wages war (vs.11; Is.11:1-5; 42:1-4; 59:15-21; 63:1-6); Jer.23:5, 6; Jn.5:22-30). His eyes are a flame of fire (see 1:14; 2:18; Dan.10:6) and many diadems (kingly dignity and Lordship) are on His head; and He has a name which no one knows except Himself (vs.12; see 2:17, also). For His robe dipped in blood, see the prophecy in Is.63:1-6; and His name is the Word of God (vs.13; Jn.1:1, 14; Col.1:19; 2:9; Mt.24:35; Is.11:1-5). For the Lord's armies in vs.14, see the commentary on 17:14. For the "sharp sword" and "rod of iron"—vs. 15, see Ps.2:8,9 and Is.11:4; Rev.1:5; 12:5); for "treading the wine press," see chapter 14:14-20; for Jesus is the Salvation Harvester, and the Conquering King and Judge against wickedness, designated by God to carry out His judgment and wrath against all unrighteousness—vs.15; 6:9-11; 16:5-7, 19; 17:5; 18:3, 24; 15:3,4; Jn.5:22-30); for He is the King of kings and Lord of lords, which appears written on His robe and thigh (vs.16; 17:14; 1:5; see also Ps.2; Jer.10:6, 7, 10; Rev.15:3,4).

An angel announces the Lord's coming conquering victory over the armies of evil on the earth ("the war of the great day of God the Almighty"—vs.17, 18; 16:14, 16). The beast and the kings of the earth assemble in war against the Lord (17:3,14; 18:3, 8-10; Zech.14:3-5,9) and the beast and the false prophet (13:1-18) were captured and thrown alive in the Lake of Fire (vss.19, 20; see Mt.25:41); and the rest of their army were killed by the sword from the mouth of the Lord (vss.21, 15; Is.11:4,5; Mt.24:27,28; Zeph.3:14-20; Ezk.43:1-9; Ps.24).

Rev.20—This chapter of the Revelation declares to us the millennial reign of Jesus Christ on the earth (vss.1-7). The certainty and length of time of these years is made known to us in that the 1000 year reign is mentioned six times in the first seven verses (vss.2-7). Satan is bound in the abyss during all these years (see the details in vss.1-3; and then released for a short time (vs.3; see commentary on 9:1 for the "abyss" and 1:18). For the "thrones and judgment" taking place in vs.4, see Dan.7:9-14, 21, 22. Those who experienced martyrdom for the Lord (6:9-11) and those who did not worship the beast, his image or take his representative mark during the Great Tribulation, came to life and reigned with Christ for the 1,000 years (vs.4; 7:14-17). This is the first resurrection, and those to be judged will be in the second resurrection (vss.5, 6). His saints (the believers) will serve Him as priests in His kingdom and reign with Him the 1,000 years (mentioned twice, in vss. 4, 6; 1:5, 6; 5:10; 1 Pet.2:9, 10).

After the 1,000 years, Satan is released for a short time to deceive the nations, Gog and Magog (reference to the nations; some say "Gog" is the leader of Magog, while some others say Gog comes from Magog or is connected with it (vss.7, 8; see Gen.10:2; Ezk.38, 39). For the "broad plain" see Ezk.38:14-23. The last attempt to wage war on the saints will be met by fire from God on their enemies and they will be devoured (vss.7-9; see the same verb here in 11:5 under similar conditions) and the devil will be casted into the Lake of Fire, and tormented there day and night forever and ever (vs.10). For the "beloved city," see Ps.48 and Ps.87; (vs.9).

Now we see the final judgment for all time to take place. The dead from land and sea, death and Hades (for which see the commentary on 1:18) are given up and come before "the great white throne" (vss.11-13; 4:2; Dan.7:9, 10). Note they are judged by (according to) their deeds (vss.12, 13) and if their name is in the book of life (see 21:27, the "Lamb's book of life," i.e., belonging to Him, His people—3:4, 5; Lk.10:20; Jn.1:12, 13; 5:24; Phil.4:3). Anyone not found in the book of life was thrown into the Lake of Fire, with death and Hades, the second death (vss.14, 15; Mt.25:41-46; Jn.10:10, 27-30; 17:3; see the Prayer in back of the book).

Rev.21—John now receives the fourth and last of his visions for the Book of Revelation (vs.10). God's family for eternity is now complete (Lk.20:34-36) and He has prepared a city for them to dwell in and live with Him forever (vss.2, 3; see the Architect and Builder in Heb.11:10, 16 and that commentary). The judgments are finished and now God has created a new heaven and new earth and new Jerusalem for them to dwell in with Him forever (vss.1, 2).

Whether the new heaven and earth are brand new or the old restored has been discussed both ways. Peter's language appears to present a restored (purified) heaven and earth (2 Pet.3:10-13) and 2 Cor.5:17 uses the same root word in "passed away" with only a different prefix regarding the spiritual birth. Heb.12:27 seemed to point this way, also (see the prophecy in Is.65:17-23). From the beginning, God's heart has always been to dwell with His people (Family—Gen.1:27, 28; 3:8; 9:7; Ex.25:8; Lev.26:11, 12). Finally, after much patience (long-suffering) by God and purification of mankind and heaven and earth (1 Pet.1:17-21; Rev.12:7, 8; 19:20; 20:10), it all comes together and takes place (vss.2, 3, 7), and much to the comfort of His Family, who shared in the sufferings of the Lord they served, but not ever to see the likes of those sufferings and pains, including physical death, ever again (vs.4; 7:14-17; Is.25:6-9; 35:10; 51:11; 65:17-23; Jn.16:22; 17:20-24). For the Lord makes (present tense) all things new (vs.5; if restoration is seen in vs.1, then that would take on the meaning that the "things" of the earth and heaven passed away, much like the "elements" being burned by fire Peter refers to in 2 Pet.3:10, 12). God wants everyone to know that these words of His are faithful and true (vs.5). The saying "it is done" in vs.6 is actually plural, meaning "they are done" (what great planning by God! see Is.25:1; 46:8-11; Eph.1:7-12), and all given to the believers (His Family) as a free gift, like His salvation to mankind (Jn.1:12, 13; 3:16, 17), which includes being a son of God (vss.6-8; Is.55:1-5; Jn.7:37-39).

One of the angels who had one of the last plagues (Rev.16) next takes John in the Spirit to a great high mountain and shows him God's new and holy city Jerusalem, coming down out of heaven and having the glory of God (vss.9, 10; Ezk.40:2). Its brilliance was like a jewel of crystal-clear jasper (vs.11; see the commentary on 4:3). From now until vs.22, the concentration of John's vision is on the city itself, the wall

and its foundation stones, and the cities gates (vss.12, 15-17, 19). The wall is great and high with twelve gates, three facing each direction (north, south, east and west), having twelve angels, and the name of the twelve tribes of Israel written on the gates (vss.12, 13). The wall has twelve foundation stones, with the twelve names of the twelve apostles of the Lamb on them (vs.14; the beautiful descriptions are given in vss.19-21). An angel was taking the measurements of the city, its gates and wall, using human measurements, which are also angelic measurements ("which the angel was using" (NIV), vss.15, 17). The city made of pure gold, like clear glass (vs.18), is laid out as a square (or others have said, by the description, a cube—length, width and height being equal, the Greek word here "four cornered"—vs.16; see 1 Kg.6:20). The city measured out to be about 1,500 miles (about half the distance, east to west, of the United States, vs.16) and the material of the wall was jasper (vs.18; 4:3), seventy-two yards long (New American Standard Bible, almost three-quarters of a football field—vs.17); and the city was pure gold, like clear glass (vs.18). Here are the twelve foundation stones that decorate the wall of the New Jerusalem (taken from Unger's Bible Dictionary): 1) jasper—colored translucent (light passes through but now transparent) varieties of quartz; sky-blue, green or rosy hues, as examples; see

4:3; 2) sapphire—an opaque stone that can come in a variety of colors, usually occurring as dark blue or different shades of blue; second in hardness to diamonds; 3) chalcedony—a greenish or bluish green silicate (glassy mineral found in various forms of quartz, opal or sand) of copper, found in mines at Chalcedon (northern Turkey); 4) emerald—usually a bright green color; 5) sardonyx—derived from two words—sard (like sardius, the next word in order) meaning a reddish-orange color; and onyx—a striped or clouded coloring, which can look off-white with striped colors; 6) sardius—a deep red or brown-red (including orange or orange-like color) varieties of chalcedony (silicate copper); 7) chrysolite—commonly topaz today, a variety of yellowish gems; 8) beryl—a hard mineral that can appear as deep varieties of green, as an emerald, or aquamarine (turquoise, sea-green) in color; 9) topaz—a variety of yellowish gems, peridot (yellowish-green), being one example; 10) chrysoprase—a light green chalcedony (word means "gold leek," like a green onion); 11) jacinth—reddish-orange or red-brown color; some have "hyacinth" here, like a blue in the sapphire; and 12) amethyst—purple or violet variety of quartz; there are few purple gemstones (Unger); see the "breastplate" jewels of Aaron in Ex.28:17-20.

The twelve gates were twelve pearls, each gate a single pearl, and the streets are as the city (vs.18)—pure gold like transparent glass (vs.21).

The city has no temple, for the Lord God Almighty and the Lamb are the temple (vs.22; see Jn.2:19; Is.66:1, 2). The light of the city will be the glory of the Lord, and its lamp is the Lamb (vs.23; see Ps.119:105; Prov.6:20-23; Jn.1:5, 9; 8:12). The nations now will walk by the light of the Lord (Is.60:3-5) and the kings of the earth will now bring their glory into it (Ps.72:10, 11, 18, 19), as the gates will never be closed with no more nighttime, celebrated by all God's Family (vss. 24-27; Ps.87).

Rev.22—As John comes to the completion of what he is shown about the New Jerusalem, the angel (21:9, 10) shows him a river of the water of life, clear as crystal, coming from the throne of God and the Lamb (vs.1). The "tree of life" was then seen on either side of the river, as the river traveled down the middle of the street (vs.2). The "tree of life" is bearing twelve kinds of fruit, yielding it's fruit every month, serving as healing for the nations (vs.21; "healing" here meaning life-giving health and nutrition for the people; see Gen.2:9, 16, 17; 3:22; note, couldn't eat off of both trees and live in Gen.2:16, 17). The setting here seems very similar to the setting in Ezk.47, yet, lets note some important distinguishing differences between them: In the millennial setting of the temple in Jerusalem (Ezk.40-48), in Ezk.47:7, 12, it states that "all kinds of trees" were located on the riverbank, while in Rev.22:2, the word "tree" of life, mentioned twice, is singular both times. One might wonder how such beautiful pure water could be existing in these two different places at two different times (the millennium and the new Jerusalem coming down out of heaven)? The answer is because God's throne is in <u>both</u> places, where the beautiful clear water comes from—the very throne of God (Ezk.43:1-9; Rev.22:1-3); and also in Gen.3:22, the "tree of life" was meant for those in the eternal state (i.e. would not die— Gen.2:16, 17; Rev.21:4), and so, after man sinned, he would be lost from God if taking this fruit in his fallen state (Gen.3:22-24); and yet instead, God set out His plan to save him (Gen.3:15), so that he could live forever with God, as He intended from the very beginning (Gen.3:8; 2:9, 16, 17; Lev. 26:11, 12).

The curse will be gone forever in the new Jerusalem (21:4) and God's throne and the Lamb will then be in it, with His bond-servants serving Him forever (vss.3, 5; 1:6; 5:9, 10; 7:14-17). And God's Family, being with Him forever (vs.3; 21:3, 7), will see God's face, with His name of ownership on their foreheads (vs.4; see 3:12; 14:1; Job 19:25, 26; Ps.16:7-11; 27:4; 84:4; Jn.3:16, 17; see the Prayer in back of the book); and with no more nighttime, God's Family will live by the light of the Lord—His glory!—and will reign with Him—their everlasting God and King—forever and ever (vs.5; 21:23-25; 19:16; Zeph.3:14-20; Is.9:6,7; Rev.1:8; 15:3,4).

The Book of Revelation closes with similar declarations, and encouragements as the book began. The faithfulness and truth of God's word are affirmed once again in vs.6 as stated in 21:5 (see also 19:11, 13). This follows supernaturally spoken through His prophets and sent angels to give to His servants what He wants them to know (Heb.12:9)—here, the things (literally) necessary to occur quickly (i.e., when they take place, they will occur quickly—vs.6, similar to Jesus' statement of His coming quickly—vs.7, 12, 20; and so to be ready, Mt.24:42, 44), and keep (heed) the words of the Book of Revelation (vs.7; 1:3; 16:15; 21:5-7). John's response to the angel is similar to his one previously in 19:10 (vss.8, 9; see that verse and commentary).

Unlike the Book of Daniel which many prophecies referred to the end times and were "sealed" up then (Dan.8:26; 12:4,

9), John was told not to seal up the words of this prophecy, for the time is near (vs.10; see commentary on 1:3 for this; 10:7-11). For understanding of vs.11, see Ezk.3:27; Dan.12:10; Rev.6:15-17; 14:6-12. The Lord will reward every man according to the work he has done (vs.12; 1 Cor.3:11-15; Eph.6:8; Rev.2:23; 20:12; Mt.16:27), as the Lord sees all things, the One who is the first and the last, the beginning and the end (vs.13; 1:8, 17; 2:8; 21:6). For "washing their robes," see the commentary on 7:14; also see Is.1:18; Acts 2:38, 39; 22:16; Heb.9:11-14; so that they will be allowed to the "tree of life" (22:2) and may enter the gates of the New Jerusalem (vss.14, 15; 21:12).

John reminds and confirms that these things have been sent by Jesus through His angel to testify these things to the churches (vs.16; 1:1, 11). For "offspring of David," see 1 Chr.17:9-14; Is.9:6, 7; Mt.1:1; Lk.1:31-33; Rev.5:5; and for "the bright and morning star," see Mt.24:27, 30; 2 Pet.1:19; Rev.22:16. The invitation in the Book of Revelation to come to know the Lord Jesus, is given with a call by the Holy Spirit and the church—the bride of Christ—along with those who read and hear the words of this book (1:3), to those who are "thirsty" (for God's life and fulfillments) and whoever wishes to receive His gift of "the water of life" (note) without cost, to come to know and follow Him (vs.17; Jn.3:16, 17; 7:37-39; 6:50, 51; 11:25, 26; Is.55:1,2; Rev.21:6; 22:1, 2; see the Prayer in the back of the book). One is strictly warned not to add to or subtract from this prophecy, with the consequences written if such is done. God has given such warnings before not to add to or subtract from His word and commandments (Dt.4:2; 12:32; Prov.30:5, 6; see also Ps.12:6; 19:7-11).

John closes by giving his affirmation to Jesus' declaration that He comes quickly (see commentary on vs.6), and so John says, "Amen" to that; "Come Lord Jesus" (vs.20); and extends the encouragement that the grace of the Lord Jesus be with all (vs.21; 1:3-5).

Bibliography

Arndt, William F; Gingrich, F. Wilbur; Bauer, Walter; and Danker, Frederick W. A Greek-English Lexicon of the New Testament and Other Early Christian Literature. Chicago and London: The University of Chicago Press, 1979.

Strong, James. Strong's Exhaustive Concordance of the Bible. Public Domain.

Unger, Merrill F. The New Unger's Bible Dictionary. Harrison, R.K., Edit; Vos, Howard F, and Barber, Cyril J., Contrib. Edit. Chicago: Moody Press, 1988.

Vine, W.E. Vine's Expository Dictionary of New Testament Words. Nashville, TN: Thomas Nelson, Inc.; 1940.

All reprints used by permission of the publishers or are public domain.

Prayer

If you have never had this relationship before and desire to know Jesus and invite Him into your life, I encourage you to pray this prayer sincerely from your heart:

"Dear Lord Jesus...Thank You for coming to earth and being faithful to the Father, fulfilling the Old Testament Scriptures written about You. Thank You for dying for my sins and rising from the dead so I may receive Your gifts of eternal life and the Holy Spirit. I now turn from my sins and leave them at the cross that You died on for me. I ask You to come into my life as my Savior and Lord. Make my life what You want me to be and help me establish good relationships with other Christians. I will serve You as my Lord and King, now and forever in Your Kingdom that will never end. Amen."

If you prayed this prayer from your heart, seek out a good Bible believing and teaching church. Ask God to bring you together with good fellow Christian relationships and to help you grow and serve your Savior and Lord. Read the Bible every day for guidance and spiritual nourishment. Spend time praying and share your new found relationship with Jesus with others also, so that they may come to know the Creator, Savior and Lord of the universe, too.

The Family Bible Studies Series

Book 1—The Family of God—Foundation. Presents the character and functions of the Trinity and eight practical Bible studies throughout the Bible on a characteristic of God (Provider, Protector, our Guide in life, Giver of all good things, etc. 35 Pages.

Book 2—The Levels of Relationships. Provides Biblical understanding about the foundational words of relationships (stranger, acquaintance, friend, companion (three kinds in the Bible), etc. and how to determine if a relationship is growing or not. 48 pages.

Book 3—Growing In God's Wisdom. Gives definitions to the Hebrew words of the introduction to the Book of Proverbs, verses 1-7, and practical application of how to pray for these "ingredients" of God's wisdom. 102 pages.

Book 4—The Theology of the Bible—The Family of God. Presents the theme of the Bible, The Family of God, from Genesis 1 to Revelation 22; plus a Biblical outline and summary of the Creation Passage of Genesis 1 and 2. 41 pages.

Book 5—The New Testament Commentary for The Family Bible Studies Series. 465 pages.

Book 6—The Book of Revelation Commentary.

CPSIA information can be obtained
at www.ICGtesting.com
Printed in the USA
BVHW041204060519
547459BV00009B/1354/P

9 781973 660354